BACKPACK EXPLORER

DISCOVERING TREES

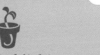

Storey Publishing

Are You Ready to DISCOVER TREES?

The world is full of all kinds of trees. Tall, small, blooming, leafy, or covered in needles, trees are waiting nearly anywhere you look. Grab this book, head outside, and get ready to meet some new friends in your neighborhood.

THINGS TO BRING ON A TREE WALK

Pencil or pen and this book

Backpack

Water bottle

Bug spray

Sunscreen

Binoculars

Camera

Snacks

CHIPS

HOW TO HAVE FUN WITH THIS BOOK!

Climb a TREE

Find SEEDS and FRUIT on trees

Go on a SCAVENGER HUNT

Look at BARK up close

Make a LEAF MASK

Learn about different LEAVES

Meet your NEIGHBORHOOD TREES

TREE WALK BADGES

There are 12 badge stickers in the back of the book that match **I SEE IT!** circles on some of the pages. When you see a type of tree or something that matches an item on the page, put the sticker on the matching **I SEE IT!** circle. See how many you can find!

Place the sticker on the circle!

I SEE IT!

Pinecones

Pine trees and other evergreens don't grow flowers or fruit. Instead, they grow rough cones to protect their seeds. A cone keeps its scales closed tight while it grows on a branch. When it is old enough, it dries out and opens up so the seeds can fall out. Keep your eyes out for cones on the ground.

Squirrels nibble on pinecones to eat the seeds.

How many types of **CONES** can you find?

Can you find a tiny cone? What about a long skinny one?

Alder

Cedar

Ponderosa pine

Eastern white pine

Sugar pine

Douglas fir

Larch

Beware! Some cones are prickly to touch!

Redwood

Blue spruce

Closer Look

When you find a pinecone, pull the scales apart and see if you can find the seeds inside.

17

Tree Discovery TIPS

NOTICE THE SIZE, SHAPE, AND FEEL of a tree's leaves and bark. Those are clues to help identify it.

LISTEN QUIETLY. Can you hear leaves rustling or branches creaking?

FOLLOW YOUR NOSE! Sniff out sweet-smelling blossoms and sticky sap.

SIT DOWN AND TAKE A BREAK under the shade of a tree.

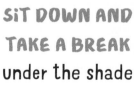

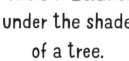

Leaves

Trees don't eat meals like people do.
Instead, they use their leaves to turn sunlight
into food. Leaves come in all kinds of shapes
and sizes. They can be long and thin or
rounded like a spoon. Some are tiny and
some are bigger than your head!

The process
of turning light
into food is called
photosynthesis
[foh-toh-SIHN-
thuh-sihs].

White ash tree

What kinds of **LEAVES** can you find?

Sycamore maple

Aspen

Beech

Birch

Ash

Can you find a heart-shaped leaf? A round one?

Chestnut

Weeping willow

Tulip

White oak

Did you see any leaves starting to change color?

Magnolia

Ginkgo

Norway maple

White mulberry

Linden

Closer Look

Hold a leaf up to the light. Can you see its veins? How many can you count?

LEAF SHAPE & COLOR

You can find all sorts of leaves on trees, at your feet, and even blowing in the wind! Check off each kind you find.

☐ Dried up

☐ Full of holes

☐ Smooth edges

☐ Yellow

☐ Red

☐ Multicolored

☐ Lobed (rounded)

☐ Compound (many parts)

☐ Jagged edges

WHY LEAVES CHANGE COLORS

Every autumn you can watch deciduous trees turn from green to bright yellow and orange before their leaves fall to the ground. ***But why do they change?***

LESS SUNLIGHT

Well, trees take in sunlight to make food, right? Their leaves have something called **chlorophyll** [CLAW-roh-fihl] that can change light into food. It's also what makes leaves green! But as the days grow colder and there is less sunlight, the leaves stop making new food. All that green chlorophyll disappears.

As the green fades, you can see the yellow and orange colors that were hiding there all along!

Enjoy the beautiful fall colors while they last!

Maple Trees

You'll know maples by their winged seeds, which look like little helicopter propellers, and by the way their leaves change colors in the fall. But sugar maples give us something really special — maple syrup! People collect the tree's watery sap and boil it down to make the thick and sticky syrup you pour on pancakes.

The red maple is the most common tree in the United States!

Do you have **MAPLE TREES** in your neighborhood?

Sugar maple

It takes 40 gallons of sap to make one gallon of syrup!

Striped maple

Norway maple

A maple's winged seed is called a **samara** [suh-MAH-rah].

Mountain maple

The edges of maple leaves are jagged.

Japanese maple

Silver maple

Red maple

Look for helicopter seed pods under a maple tree. See how the seed is attached to a long thin wing? Throw it high in the air and watch it spin down!

Closer Look

WHAT KiND OF TREE iS iT?

Notice how each tree has its own special look. It takes time to learn the details of each tree, but it's easy to tell what basic group it belongs in. There are two main types of trees — coniferous and deciduous.

iS iT CONiFEROUS?
[CAW-NiH-FUHR-UHS]

Coniferous trees, or conifers, have skinny needles instead of broad leaves. Most never drop their needles, which keeps them looking bushy and green even in winter. Conifers grow their seeds in special cones that are easy to find on the ground.

iS iT DECiDUOUS?
[DiH-SiHD-JUH-WUHS]

Aspens, oaks, maples, and other deciduous trees drop their leaves every fall. Before they drop, most of those leaves turn from green to bright and fiery red, orange, and yellow.

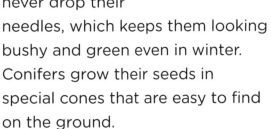

Weeping willow

Southern magnolia

White birch

Chestnut

Bactris palm

Bald cypress

Remember the **C RULE**: Conifers have cones!

Incense cedar

Douglas fir

Giant sequoia

Coast redwood

Conifers

I SEE IT!

Firs and spruces are different kinds of conifers. Here's a way to tell them apart: Spruce needles are square and spiky, but fir needles are flat and friendly!

Most conifers stay green all year, which is why they are called "evergreen" trees.

What other **EVERGREENS** can you find?

Balsam fir

Do you like the smell of evergreen trees?

White pine

Eastern red cedar

Can you feel sticky sap on the bark?

Blue spruce

Hemlock

Closer Look

When you look at needles, notice if the ends are pointed or more rounded. Are the undersides dark green or pale?

WHY WE NEED TREES

We depend on trees for many things that we use every day. Take a look!

FURNITURE

FIREWOOD

SYRUP

PAPER & BOOKS

FRUIT

NUTS

BUILDINGS

SHADE

PLAY

TREES HELP CLEAN THE AIR

Most important of all, trees recycle the air for us and keep it clean. Thanks, trees!

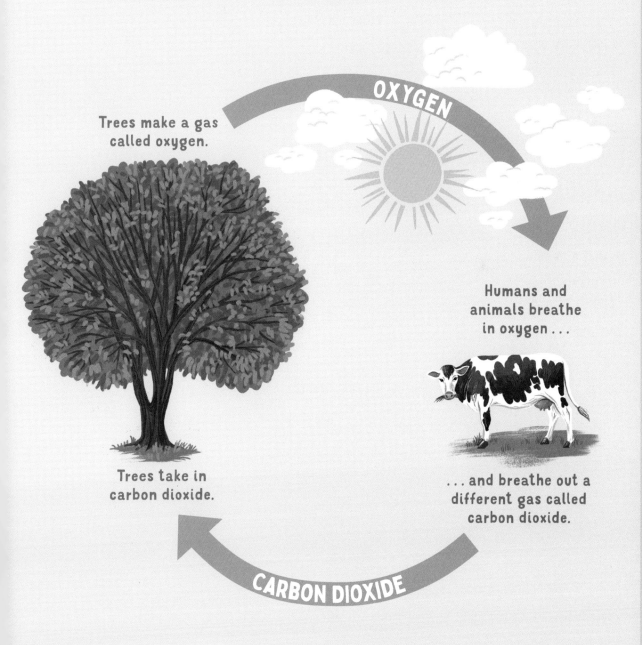

OXYGEN

Trees make a gas called oxygen.

Humans and animals breathe in oxygen . . .

. . . and breathe out a different gas called carbon dioxide.

Trees take in carbon dioxide.

CARBON DIOXIDE

Pinecones

Pine trees and other evergreens don't grow flowers or fruit. Instead, they grow rough cones to protect their seeds. A cone keeps its scales closed tight while it grows on a branch. When it is old enough, it dries out and opens up so the seeds can fall out. Keep your eyes out for cones on the ground.

Squirrels nibble on pinecones to eat the seeds.

How many types of CONES can you find?

Alder

Cedar

Ponderosa pine

Eastern white pine

Can you find a tiny cone? What about a long skinny one?

Sugar pine

Douglas fir

Larch

Beware! Some cones are prickly to touch!

Redwood

Blue spruce

Closer Look

When you find a pinecone, pull the scales apart and see if you can find the seeds inside.

Outdoor Tree
ADVENTURE

Here are some fun ways to play with your tree friends!

BUILD A FORT

Find a large boulder, thick tree trunk, or fallen tree to use as a "wall." The side of a building works, too!

Collect a bunch of long sticks and fallen branches from the ground. Lean the branches against your wall, making sure there is enough space to sit underneath.

Fill in the gaps. Collect smaller sticks and leaves to weave between the larger branches.

Crawl inside! Eat a snack, read a book, listen for bird calls, or tell a story inside your new hideaway.

CLIMB A TREE

Ask an adult to help you find a tree with sturdy, low-hanging branches. Leafy trees like oaks are good for climbing.

Use your strong arms to pull yourself up onto a thick branch. Ask an adult for help if you need a boost!

Stay safe. As you climb, think of the rule of three: Two hands and a foot, or two feet and one hand on the tree at all times!

JUMP IN A PILE OF LEAVES!

This one is easy! Grab a rake and make a big pile of crunchy fallen leaves. Now take a running leap and dive right in!

Aspen Trees

You'll know an aspen tree by its unusual whitish-colored trunk. But the coolest thing about a group (or **grove**) of aspens is that they are all connected to each other underground. What looks like a bunch of different trees is actually one huge tree that shares the same set of roots.

Some aspen groves are many thousands of years old.

Quaking aspen

Which of these **ASPEN COUSINS** can you find?

Eastern cottonwood

Quaking aspen

Have you ever seen cottonwood seed fluff falling like snow?

White poplar

Weeping willow

Willow trees like to grow near water.

Closer Look

Look at an aspen trunk. See how the bark of a young tree is pale with dark markings? Do you think they look like eyes?

PARTS OF A TREE

The **crown** or **canopy** is the top of the tree.

lobe

vein

stem

Leaves provide food for the tree.

Branches grow from the trunk.

The **trunk** is like the stem of the tree.

Roots hold the tree to the ground and absorb water.

22

BARK HUNT

Look for different types of tree bark. How do they feel when you touch them? Check off each kind you find.

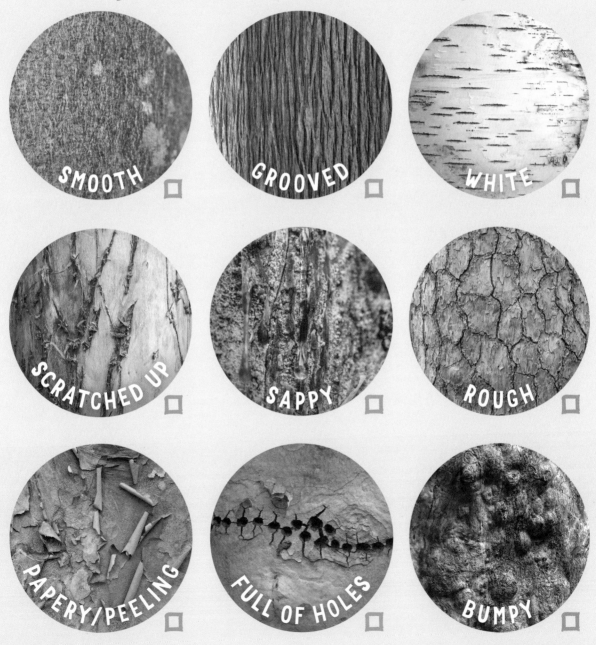

SMOOTH ☐

GROOVED ☐

WHITE ☐

SCRATCHED UP ☐

SAPPY ☐

ROUGH ☐

PAPERY/PEELING ☐

FULL OF HOLES ☐

BUMPY ☐

Logs and Stumps

You may feel it's sad to see a big tree fall over, but it can actually be good for a forest. When a tall tree falls, it leaves an open space so more sunlight can reach the ground and help baby trees grow. Rotting logs and stumps feed the soil and make great homes for all sorts of insects and mushrooms!

Bears, raccoons, and other animals often pull apart rotting logs to look for insects to eat.

Look for **LOGS AND STUMPS** on your walks.

Mushrooms and fungus help break down an old stump.

What can you find growing on an old, crumbling log?

Many insects live in fallen trees. Can you see any?

Closer Look

Fallen logs and stumps help other plants grow. Take a close look at one. Do you see any moss? What about ferns or fungus or new tree seedlings?

Bark

When you see a tree, feel its bark. Is it bumpy or smooth? Scaly or rough? Gray or yellow or brown? Each type of tree has its own special kind of bark. Bark is a little like your skin. It helps protect the tree from bad weather, disease, and damage from animals and insects.

Some bark is almost as smooth as paper. Other types are bumpy or have deep grooves you can stick your finger into.

What kinds of **BARK** do you see?

Honey locust

White pine

Look out for sticky sap dripping down!

Honey locusts have spiky thorns growing on their bark!

Red cedar

Yellow birch

Have you ever seen bark peeling off a tree?

Closer Look

Can you find holes in a tree trunk? How many? How big and deep are they? What do you think made them?

Make a
TREE RUBBING

Make a memory of your tree with a colorful work of art. You'll need some plain white paper, masking tape, and a pencil or crayon.

BARK RUBBING

You can do this activity any time of year, even in winter!

1 Find a tree with interesting bark. Spread your paper against its trunk and tape it in place.

2 Rub your pencil or crayon over the whole paper using gentle pressure to show the pattern of the bark.

Check out all the little details on your rubbing!

LEAF RUBBING

It's best to use green summer leaves for this activity.

1 Gather some leaves of different shapes and sizes.

2 Spread a leaf out on a flat surface, bottom side up.

3 Place your paper over the leaf, and gently rub the side of a crayon over the paper. Make sure you rub over the entire leaf.

4 When you have a complete rubbing of one leaf, grab a new leaf and a different color crayon and make another.

NOTE: *You can make a cool picture with needles from a pine, fir, or juniper tree, too!*

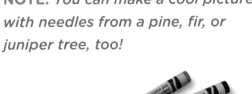

Flowering Trees

I SEE IT!

Many trees grow flowers in the spring. These blossoms are often pink or white, and can be as small as your thumb or as big as your head. When bees and other critters poke around looking for nectar to drink, they move dusty pollen from one blossom to another. This is called **pollination** [pol-luh-NAY-shuhn], and it helps flowers make seeds. The wind helps pollinate, too!

Tulip magnolia trees have blossoms as big as your hand!

Are there any **FLOWERING TREES** near you?

Tulip tree

Eastern redbud

Chestnut

Do you notice that each flowering tree has a special smell?

Crab apple

Lilac

Dogwood

Watch how petals fall like snow when the wind blows.

Jacaranda

Closer Look

Look closely at a tree flower. How many petals does it have? Do you see any orange or yellow pollen inside?

FROM SEED TO TREE

Follow along with the pictures below to see how a tree grows.

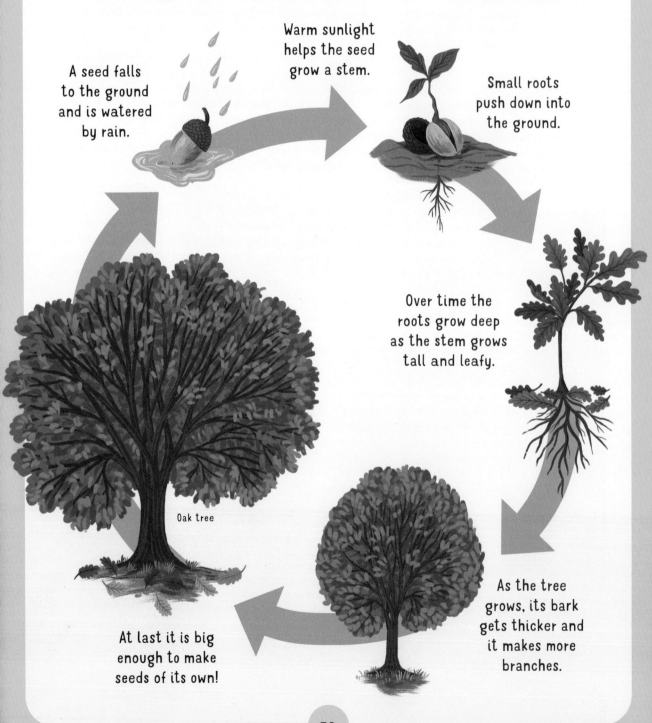

A seed falls to the ground and is watered by rain.

Warm sunlight helps the seed grow a stem.

Small roots push down into the ground.

Over time the roots grow deep as the stem grows tall and leafy.

Oak tree

As the tree grows, its bark gets thicker and it makes more branches.

At last it is big enough to make seeds of its own!

TREE RING DETECTIVE!

As a tree grows taller, its trunk becomes thicker and stronger to support new branches. For every year it grows, it produces a new trunk ring. If you find a cut stump, you can count its rings to learn how old it was — one ring for every year it grew!

A large space between rings shows a good year for growing!

These scars show where branches broke off.

Two rings close together means the tree didn't grow much that year.

Fruit Trees

Some trees give us delicious fruit to eat. The fruit grows around the seeds of the tree. Apples and pears have several small seeds inside each piece of fruit, while peaches and plums have one large seed inside a hard pit. Birds and other animals love to eat fruit. They help new trees grow when they poop out those seeds later in new places!

Apple tree

There are over 7,500 different types of apples in the world!

What kinds of **FRUIT TREES** can you find?

Cherry

Mulberry

Plum

Pear

Peaches are called stone fruits because their pits look like small rocks.

Peach

Persimmon

Mango

Apple

Lime

Lemon

Grapefruits, oranges, lemons, and limes are called citrus fruits.

Grapefruit

Tangerine

Orange

Closer Look

Open up a fruit and count the seeds inside! How many are there? What shape are the seeds?

Leaf MATH

You can find leaves, seeds, needles, and pinecones nearly anywhere outside. Take a walk to collect some interesting finds, making sure you only pick up items from the ground. Then take a seat and start sorting!

SORT BY COLOR

Divide your tree treasures by color. Put red with red, green with green, and so on. Try arranging your color piles in rainbow order.

SORT BY SIZE OR SHAPE

If you found a bunch of one type of leaf, try lining them up by size, from smallest to biggest. If you found lots of different kinds of leaves, sort them into different piles according to their shape: oval leaves in one pile, hand-shaped leaves in another.

MAKE PATTERNS

Get creative and set out your leaves in neat patterns using different colors or shapes. Can you make a checkerboard design using two types of leaf?

CONE COUNT AND NEEDLE LINES

If you're surrounded by conifer trees, count all the cones you find on the ground! Or collect needles and stretch them out in long skinny lines. How about using them to write numbers on the ground?

Nut Trees

Many humans and other animals love to eat nuts. They are good for you and make tasty snacks. In the fall, squirrels and chipmunks gather nuts from all kinds of trees to store away and eat through the winter. They bury so many, they forget about some! The ones they forget may grow into new trees.

Buckeye tree

Some nuts, like buckeyes, aren't safe to eat. Never eat nuts that you find on the ground.

Have you seen any of these **NUTS** growing?

Pistachios

Horse chestnuts (buckeyes)

Nuts protected by a hard outer shell are called true nuts.

Almonds

Nuts are a kind of seed.

Squirrels have very sharp teeth for biting through shells.

Acorns

Pecan

Walnuts look like little brains!

Chestnuts

Black walnuts

Closer Look

Many nuts are protected by an outer shell or layer. Chestnut shells are spiky!

Make a
NATURE
MASK

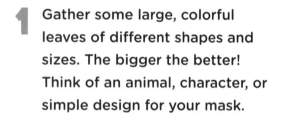

Get wild with a colorful leaf mask! You'll need a pair of scissors and a permanent marker.

1 Gather some large, colorful leaves of different shapes and sizes. The bigger the better! Think of an animal, character, or simple design for your mask.

TIP: Sometimes it helps to dry the leaves and press them flat under a heavy book for a day or two.

2 Cut out eye holes and decorate your leaf. Will your mask have pointy ears like a fox or a beak like an owl? What about whiskers, spots, or stripes?

NOTE: If you can't find leaves big enough for a mask, try making little leaf animals instead. Arrange different sizes and shapes of leaves to make spiky hedgehogs, fluffy bird chicks, or scaly fish!

Seeds

Even the tallest trees start off as little seeds. A seed holds everything a new tree needs to grow, if it gets enough sunlight and water to sprout. Seeds come in all sorts of shapes and sizes. Trees can't move, so they depend on animals, water, and wind to move their seeds around.

Some seeds wait many years before sprouting into a tree.

Tatar maple

What kinds of **SEEDS** can you find?

Ash

Peach

Elm

Some tiny seeds catch a ride in animal fur!

Black locust

Maple

Alder

Seed pods dry up and split open to let the seeds out.

American sweetgum

Birch

Sycamore

Can you find some sort of seed shell or pod on the ground? Open up the tough outside layer and look for the seeds inside. What shape are they?

Closer Look

TREE SCENTS

Let your nose lead the way! Cozy up to different kinds of trees and see if you can smell some of these things:

☐ Pine sap

☐ Fir needles

☐ Blooming flowers

☐ Ripe berries

☐ Fruit

☐ Rotting wood

☐ Mushrooms

☐ Dried leaves

☐ Fallen nuts

See a TREE BREATHE

Leaves breathe like people do! Have you ever breathed on a window and fogged up the glass? That fog is the water vapor from your breath. To see how leaves do this too, grab a large clear plastic bag and twist tie and find a leafy tree!

1 Look for a branch in direct sunlight. Pull your bag over the end of a branch, putting as many leaves inside as you can.

2 Use the twist tie to tie off the open end of the bag so no air can escape.

3 Check on your bag at the end of the day. Is it fogged up inside? Can you see drops of water on the sides? Is there a small puddle at the bottom of the bag? That's the moisture breathed out by the tree!

NOTE: *Don't forget to take the bag off the tree when your experiment is done.*

Oak Trees

If you see a tree with acorns, you know you're looking at an oak. There are many types of oaks in North America, and most of them grow to be large trees. Oak wood is strong and is often used to make furniture like tables and chairs. Many oaks have long leaves with several lobes that can be pointed or rounded.

Oak trees can live to be more than 100 years old.

Have you seen any of these different **OAKS?**

Southern live oak

White oak

White oaks have rounded edges on their leaves.

Blackjack oak

Red oak and pin oak leaves have pointy edges.

Red oak

Pin oak

Every few years, oak trees produce an extra-large crop of acorns.

Burr oak

Can you collect different types of acorns? Look closely at their little caps.

Closer Look

HUG A TREE!

Trees keep the world alive, and that's hard work. They stand in storms and snow and under the hot sun, helping other creatures survive.

The next time you see a tree, walk up and give it a hug!

Can you get both your arms around it? If the trunk is wide, grab a friend or two, stretch out and hold hands for a group hug!

Thank You, TREE!

48

MY DAY OF DISCOVERING TREES

Match up stickers to what you saw on your tree walk.

Found some seeds or nuts

Counted some conifers

Picked up a few leaves

Looked around a fallen log

Pinecones

A flowering tree

A tree with fruit

Red leaves

So many different shapes and sizes!

Yellow leaves

MY LIST OF TREES

Keep a list of the trees you find.

Tree name: _____ Date/Time: _____

Where I saw it: _____

What I noticed about it: _____

Tree name: _____ Date/Time: _____

Where I saw it: _____

What I noticed about it: _____

Tree name: _____ Date/Time: _____

Where I saw it: _____

What I noticed about it: _____

Tree name: _____ Date/Time: _____

Where I saw it: _____

What I noticed about it: _____

Tree name: _____ Date/Time: _____

Where I saw it: _____

What I noticed about it: _____

Tree name: _____ Date/Time: _____

Where I saw it: _____

What I noticed about it: _____

I saw this tree:

Draw a picture of a tree that you saw on your tree walk.

Draw a leaf, cone, or seed from your tree here.

Douglas fir

Southern magnolia

Larch

Incense cedar

Weeping willow

Apple

Ginkgo

Oak

Coast redwood

Cottonwood

Crab apple

Blue spruce

Chestnut

Giant sequoia

Quaking aspen

White birch

Bald cypress

Apple

Incense cedar

Cherry

Vine maple

Birch

Sweetleaf

Blackjack oak

Horse chestnut

Douglas fir

Acorn

Burr oak

Ash

Yellowwood

Ohio buckeye

Cedar

Mulberry

Spruce

Bigleaf maple

Ginkgo

Red buckeye

Walnut

White oak

Sweetgum

Apple

Horse chestnut

Blue spruce

Redbud

Dogwood

Red oak

TREE BADGE STICKERS

Look for these types of trees or tree-related things. When you spot one, place your badge on the matching page where it says, "I SEE IT!"

LEAVES, page 4

MAPLE TREES, page 8

CONIFERS, page 12

PINECONES, page 16

ASPEN TREES, page 20

LOGS AND STUMPS, page 24

BARK, page 26

FLOWERING TREES, page 30

FRUIT TREES, page 34

NUT TREES, page 38

SEEDS, page 42

OAK TREES, page 46

The mission of Storey Publishing is to serve our customers by
publishing practical information that encourages
personal independence in harmony with the environment.

Text by Kathleen Yale
Edited by Deanna F. Cook and Lisa H. Hiley
Art direction and book design by Jessica Armstrong
Text production by Jennifer Jepson Smith

Illustrations by © Oana Befort
Interior photography by Mars Vilaubi © Storey Publishing LLC, 5 (ash, aspen, beech, birch, ginkgo, white mulberry, Norway maple, white oak), 9 (mt. maple, red maple, striped maple), 23 smooth, 28, 29, 36, 37 ex. b., 40, 41 ex. bkgrd. t.l., 45 b.

Additional photography by © aarrows/iStock.com, 23 white; © Alfio Scisetti/Alamy Stock Photo, 21 quaking aspen; © alias612/stock.adobe.com, 5 chestnut; © All Canada Photos/Alamy Stock Photo, 21 eastern cottonwood; © almaje/stock.adobe.com, 31 lilac; © Anastasiia Malinich/stock.adobe.com, 39 black walnut (all); © Andres Victorero/iStock.com, 39 chestnut (nuts); © Anneliese Gruenwald-Maerkl/iStock.com, 39 horse chestnut; © Avalon_Studio/iStock.com, 5 linden; © Azure-Dragon/iStock.com, 13 balsam fir twig; © baibaz/stock.adobe.com, 35 peach & pear; © Barbara/stock.adobe.com, 2 & 16; © bgfoto/iStock.com, 45 t., 47 red oak; © bjdlzx/iStock.com, 31 crab apple; © bjphotographs/stock.adobe.com, 2 & 17 sugar pine; © blickwinkel/Alamy Stock Photo, 13 hemlock; © Boarding1Now/iStock.com, 35 apple; © Branko Srot/stock.adobe.com, 30; © BreakingTheWalls/iStock.com, 5 b.r.; © Bruce Montagne/Dembinsky Photo Associates/Alamy Stock Photo, 21 eastern cottonwood leaves; © cassp/iStock.com, 31 jacaranda; © cglade/iStock.com, 7 leaves r.; © chengyuzheng/iStock.com, 35 lemon; © Chushkin/iStock.com, 2 & 17 blue spruce; © CypherOx/iStock.com, 47 b.r. © David Winger/Alamy Stock Photo, 13 blue spruce; © denira/stock.adobe.com, 35 grapefruit; © Dessas/iStock.com, 23 papery; © DianaLynne/iStock.com, 31 tulip tree; © djekill2007/stock.adobe.com, 43 peach; © Don Johnston_ON/Alamy Stock Photo, 13 white pine; © Dorling Kindersley ltd/Alamy Stock Photo, 21 white poplar leaves, 47 pin oak & blackjack oak; © DorSteffen/stock.adobe.com, 43 b.r.; © duke2015/stock.adobe.com, 13 eastern red cedar; © Elena Bezzubtseva/iStock.com, 47 white oak; © enskanto/stock.adobe.com, 2 & 17 alder; © fabrice/stock.adobe.com, 25 t.r.; © Firdes Sayilan/Dreamstime.com, 43 sycamore; © fishbgone/iStock.com, 2 & 17 Douglas fir; © fortton/stock.adobe.com, 2 & 17 cedar; © fotogal/iStock.com, 13 eastern red cedar twig; © gamelover/stock.adobe.com, 48; © George Ostertag/Alamy Stock Photo, 27 red cedar; © GeorgePeters/iStock.com, 39 acorns; © Gerry/stock.adobe.com, 25 b.r.; © Grant Heilman Photography/Alamy Stock Photo, 5 weeping willow; Greg Hume/CC BY-SA 3.0/Wikimedia Commons, 27 honey locust; © H. Mark Weidman Photography/Alamy Stock Photo, 23 grooved; © Hairem/Shutterstock.com, 33; © Hakase_/iStock.com, 19 t.; © heibaihui/iStock.com, 5 magnolia; © HHelene/iStock.com, 9 flowers; © hippostudio/iStock.com, 35 persimmon; © Ian/stock.adobe.com, 23 holes; © igaguri_1/iStock.com, 38; © Irina Silayeva/stock.adobe.com, 47 southern live oak; © Island Images/Alamy Stock Photo, 13 balsam fir; © Jakub/stock.adobe.com, 9 Norway maple; © Jerry Pavia, 9 b.r., 31 b.r., 42; Jessica Armstrong © Storey Publishing LLC, 37 b., 41 bkgrd. t.l.; © john shepherd/iStock.com, 35 b.r.; © JohnGollop/iStock.com, 5 sycamore maple; © jorgeantonio/iStock.com, 27 yellow birch; © Juj Winn/Getty Images, 47 burr oak; © Julia_Sudnitskaya/iStock.com, 43 ash; © kolesnikovserg/stock.adobe.com, 5 tulip, 31 chestnut, 39 (almonds, pecans, pistachio nuts); © kristo74/iStock.com, 2 & 17 larch; © ksushsh/iStock.com, 35 tangerine; © KURJANPHOTO/iStock.com, 25 m.; © Laurence Berger/iStock.com, 25 m.r.; © Laurent Fox/Getty Images, 23 bumpy; © Le Do/stock.adobe.com, 31 eastern redbud & dogwood; © Leopardinatree/iStock.com, 39 squirrel; © LesyaD/iStock.com, 3 & foldout, wood bkgrd.; © lilkar/iStock.com, 7 b.; © Lokibaho/iStock.com, 21 b.r.; © Lorerock81/iStock.com, 39

b.r.; © Lpcornish/iStock.com, 24; © M.Khebra/Shutterstock.com, 39 pistachio branch; © Magone/iStock.com, 35 mango; © Maslov Dmitry/stock.adobe.com, 4; © Melinda Fawver/Shutterstock.com, 13 hemlock twig; © michaklootwijk/stock.adobe.com, 43 alder; © Mircea Costina/stock.adobe.com, 8; © myself/iStock.com, 23 rough; © Neydtstock/iStock.com, 9 Japanese maple; © nickkurzenko/stock.adobe.com, 2 & 17 eastern white pine; © noppharat/stock.adobe.com, 35 mulberries; © ojoel/stock.adobe.com, foldout, sky; © OlgaKot20/stock.adobe.com, 21 weeping willow leaves; © Pasticcio/iStock.com, 34; © prescott09/stock.adobe.com, 46; © PurpleImages/iStock.com, 21 weeping willow; © RooM The Agency/stock.adobe.com, 19 b.; © sasapanchenko/iStock.com, 35 cherries; © saz1977/iStock.com, 25 t.l.; © Scisetti Alfio/stock.adobe.com, 43 maple; © scisettialfio/iStock.com, 43 American sweetgum; © sequential5/iStock.com, 27 b.r.; © serebryakova/iStock.com, 35 lime; © Serghei Velusceac/stock.adobe.com, 12; © Sergi/stock.adobe.com, 18; © Silvy78/stock.adobe.com, 2 & 17 b.r.; Simon A. Eugster (Switzerland), aka. LivingShadow on Wikimedia, 43 black locust; © sladerer/Shutterstock.com, 20; © spline_x/stock.adobe.com, 43 elm; © sunnychicka/iStock.com, 21 white poplar; © tabitazn/stock.adobe.com, 35 orange; © Tevarak/iStock.com, 3 nails; © thekopmylife/iStock.com, 25 m.l.; © ti-ja/iStock.com, 23 scratched; © twinlynx/stock.adobe.com, 23 sappy, 27 white pine; © undefined undefined/iStock.com, 13 white pine twig; © underworld/Shutterstock.com, 2 & 17 ponderosa pine; © Valentyn Volkov/Alamy Stock Photo, 43 birch; © versh/iStock.com, 9 sugar maple; © Viktor/stock.adobe.com, 35 plum; © virtustudio/iStock.com, 13 b.r.; © VvoeVale/iStock.com, 9 silver maple; © WILDLIFE GmbH/Alamy Stock Photo, 13 blue spruce twig; © yenwen/iStock.com, 2 & 17 redwood; © YinYang/iStock.com, 26; © YK/stock.adobe.com, 39 chestnut branch;

Text © 2021 by Storey Publishing, LLC

Storey books are available at special discounts when purchased in bulk for premiums and sales promotions as well as for fund-raising or educational use. Special editions or book excerpts can also be created to specification. For details, please call 800-827-8673, or send an email to sales@storey.com.

Storey Publishing
210 MASS MoCA Way
North Adams, MA 01247
storey.com

Printed in China by R.R. Donnelley
10 9 8 7 6 5 4 3 2

Library of Congress Cataloging-in-Publication Data on file